Chamber With Mirrors

Nuran Barengi

Translation
Ender Gürol

Chamber With Mirrors

Nuran Barengi

Paving Ways For New Writers

First Published in India in 2015 by First Step Publishing

Editorial / Sales / Marketing Office at
303-304 Garnet Nirmal Lifestyles Ph 2
Behind Nirmal Lifestyles Mall
LBS Marg Mulund West
Mumbai 400080
E-Mail:- info@firststepcorp.com
www.firststepcorp.com

Copyright © Authors Copyright

All rights reserved. No part of this publication may be reproduced, stored in or introduced into retrieval system or transmitted in any form or by any means (electronically, mechanically, photocopying, recording or otherwise) without the prior written permission of the publisher . Any person who does an unauthorized act in relation to this publication may be liable to criminal prosecution and civil claims for damages.

ISBN: - 978-93-83306-23-7
Publisher and Managing Editor: Rohit Shetty
Branding, Marketing and Promotions by: Design Fishing
Cover Image by: Ihsan Arı.
Typeset in Book Antique
PaperBack: ₹ 180
Rest: $ 8

About the Author

Nuran Barengi:
Born in 1968, Ergani/Diyarbakır, she went to the primary school of the neighbourhood until its third year, as she had to leave her birth place because of her father's assignment to a new governmental post in Ankara where she continued her primary and secondary studies. During her graduate years she worked in the Ministry of Finance while pursuing her studies at the Faculty of Economics. The Ministry of Finance, the Treasury Undersecretariat of Prime Ministry, the General Secretariat of the Administrative Council of Public Banks and The Agricultural Bank of Turkish Republic were the organizations at which she occupied important posts, which was followed by her research work, in her capacity of a staff member, at the Economics Department of the Boğaziçi University.

During her stay in Ankara, Mrs. Barengi, took singing lessons and dabbled in jazz music, studied ballet, went into journalism, and dipped into dramatic art. Married and the mother of two children, she lives in Istanbul, Turkey.

The interest she cultivated in arts and social sciences ever since she was in her teens played a decisive role in the development of her mental framework and in her undivided attention bestowed upon current social affairs. Philosophical issues particularly steered toward concepts of universal balance, of butterfly effect and of infinity have been the basic components in the formation of her spiritual framework and contributed to the many a perplexing problem related to human relations. An observing mind, coupled with an enthusiasm to experience life profoundly unleashed in her a resolute energy resulting into poetic creations. All these tributaries converged into the formation of her character reminiscent of streams flowing into the vast main.

Prizes and Shields

1. Literary prize awarded on the World Women's Day on 8th March, 2012, on the occasion of the festival organized by World Film and Arts Foundation and the Aznavur Sanat for prominent women who have contributed meritoriously to the development of fine arts and social media.
2. Shield of gratitude offered by TUMBIAD (April 2012) for her integrating thorny social issues with art in her poem entitled Deprem

(Earthquake) dedicated to the children, victims of the Van earthquake.

3. Shield for her contribution, in her capacity of contributor, to fine arts on the occasion of the Mothers' Day, 12 May 2012, organized by the World and Anatolian Federation for Social Assistance in which took part local and foreign prominent members of the society.

4. To figure in the book entitled Gülbaranın Gülleri edited by Sedat Eroğlu, is a sincere tribute and joy for Nuran Barengi; it is a work that took the author ten long years for preparation. The book reminds the future generations that Diyarbakır-Ergani has been a center from which eminent men and women of letters, sciences and arts as well as politicians came out to contribute to the general culture of the land.

About Our Translator

Ahmet Ender Gürol

Ahmet Ender Gürol born in 1931, a prolific translator and lexicographer, has over a hundred books to his credit. Among the books he has translated from Turkish into English we can name The Time Regulation Institute; The Peace in Mind; The History of the 19th Century Turkish literature of A.H. Tanpınar; Istanbul was a Fairy Tale of Mario Levi; Locked Lives of T.Afsin Ilgar; In The Name of The Father, the Son and the Holy Spirit: A History of the Crusades, of Doğan Yurdakul; The Crimean Times of Sevim Çokum; The Frankfurt Journal of A. Haşim; and Murat IV of Turan Oflazoğlu.

Preface

Much as I would have liked to put into words my impressions of Barengi's poems, I cannot help realizing once more that a work of art speaks for itself and that words are not capable of expressing an artistic 'entity', for, be it a poem or painting, or music for that matter, it is a sort of a will-o'-the- wisp chased in vain, just like a symbol with a thousand faces. What distinguishes her art is its versatility reflected in mirrors that reflect endless combination of images summing up many a trend of modern versification.

~Ahmet Ender Gürol

*Objective projection calls for what has objective existence
Relative time and space is but a matter of perception.*

~ Nuran Barengi

Earthquake

Lasted but five minutes
Screams of despair
For the loss of papa
Scolding cold shower
On my agony reflected
In my children's eyes
That terror rent asunder
Moment branded by tremor
Ne plus ultra!
Van earthquake!
I'm suffocating!
Mourning atmosphere
Putting ice on our dolour
Why but why? why on earth
I didn't know that?
We loved so much
To verbalize!
Post-seismic disturbance
Eleventh hour picture of winter kids
Who cannot heave a sigh
Despair lacking succour

I wonder if my maternal love can temper it
If only I can have him
Look at the overall picture
With the eye 'of that kid'
If I can have my voice heard
By the child within them
Hoping that their ears will hear
If not their heart
And say: "You were a child once!"
Who knows whether I can or not
If only I could attach to my wings
The dreams of the vernal season
If only I could fly with my tortoise passion
Over all the griefs and pains
If only I could extinguish the wild fire
Sprinkling water over the wild forest
By my terror-stricken panic...
I know I can't
Yet I shall give it a try!

Pomegranate Flowers

Oh children of mine!
And in particular
My beaming daughter with seraphic looks
No, she can't possibly be roguish, can she?
I'm saving moments full of terror for the future
"I don't want to grow up, " says my daughter
I couldn't care less!
As though
Dating from millennia my childhood
My anxiousness to grow up as soon as possible
And my curiosity
To understand what said
My brother's manual on cybernetics
The comparative study of the automatic control system
Churning whirlpool when out of control
Growing placidity
The eye's accustoming to the darkness
O my Pomegranate flower of mine
We have prepared rooms with mirrors
For those roundabout and around you if any
And all our pomegranate flowers are at peace now

I'm saving moments full of terror for the future
Let them hear a mother's scream
No more room left for us to recede anymore
Let them ask us pomegranate flowers
And we shall set off from the heart to the mind
For the moment my pitiful apologies
For lives we've transformed into a ghoulish world
I'm saving moments full of terror for the future
When I look at the world through the chamber with mirrors
I am offended by mirrors
I want to meet reflections of affection in them
I'm trying
And wipe away the mirrors
That breath of fear has tarnished
For all our children
I still entertain hope
Hope there must be

A Touch Of A Butterfly

Enthusiasm we need
For a new start
For an auspicious beginning
From fonts and origin
Now that everything has finally been settled
A song emerging from the past
Or may be a scent
A touch of a butterfly
Associations with no end
Chagrin we believed consigned to oblivion
Stages unwarranted demonstrations
Hibernal reminiscences
Suddenly pervade my soul
the pain of a lacerated finger
Suddenly showers down my soul
Like the summer rain
To cope with life
And the rain stops
Pending the next déjà vu experience of
A touch of a butterfly
When the odour of the earth
Makes you conscious of the moment

The Winter Sun
I must take them off
These glasses
Over which tumble down
My tuff of hair
Should I wear a hair band, I wonder;
Or, or have it cut off altogether
For my eyes must meet the eyes
Of those happy in the hope
Viewing life with glee
Boosting up my joy
O these dark glasses
That I often misplace somewhere
Blessed relief!
Now is the time when the sun shall penetrate into me
Even though the time winter night be.

Chamber With Mirrors
I

Thoughts swarming in my brain
Surrounded by mirrors
Play squash each to each
They break
And crack
One by one
Maybe in twos or threes
Knocked into splinters
New swarm of
Solitudes
Splinter-strewn battlefield
I'm looking for
My thought that
Had first hit the mirror
Is there no end to this bloodshed?
Suppose I've found it though
So what?
Excessive, massive bleeding
Wounds all over and fractures to boot

Bravo!
O supreme painter
A work of optical treat
A self-portrait in one single stroke
A work of fine tune indeed
Mutatis mutandis
Blown to smithereens

Chamber With Mirrors
II

The same chamber with mirrors,
Lying flat on its back
In the vast sea of infinity
I am leaning my thoughts
Against the flanks of the mountain of quiescence
And picking off
With a pair of tweezers
Those marked by eager hopefulness
Leaving dormant
Those lacking in balance
Relieved I go out of the room
Oxygen takes the sting out of my cells
Pearls of hope fill my soul
A smile on my lips
And the game ends.

Imaginary Mirror

Crowded loneliness
Is it affection
Or Love
you're in pursuit of?
You can't possibly lose something
You've never had
Reflection in the mirror of the busty woman
Whose image you've never been able to draw
Deceiver that you are!
Come, recklessly face
Your life weight
You the solitary
Face to face side by side
You are off side
Give up looking for your lost love
You never had
You'll end up finding
The loneliness you try to shun
Deceitful mirror!
April 2011

Dance

Every moment that goes by
Alienates man from himself
Ill-assorted dance partners that we are
You and I you and I
I've transformed you, haven't I?
Years my confidant that keeps whispering
From crevices, chinks and clefts
Those that succeed to synchronize
The rate of rhythmic recurrence of the feet
On which we can't help stepping on the beat
Now and then now and then
So be it, what of it
Not always do our feet attune
To each other
So be it what of it
I'm ready to try it
Once more with you
O beloved!

The Vernal Dream

Someone sets a trap
I couldn't care less
I wish that he laid
The most innocent of all traps
Enveloped in dark clouds
We are wallowing in dirt
Rain cannot wash it away, no
Snow can work a cure perhaps,
No not even snow can blanket it though
It must be showered with hail
Swathed in mist blanketed by fog
The country is blighted resulting
In withering, cessation of growth,
Let an avalanche wipes us out and puts an end to us
So much the better
Is it possible that we have in the past
Been the target of more than a few
Which made us such a stupid lot
It'd be much better if men showered down on our skulls
The ground leaping up and down with excitement
The lower and the upper layers of the earth
Changing places mutually

Packed snow that melts slowly in the sun
Yielding water fructifying the earth
O masters of the Earth
Time to sow your finest poems now
It is now spring.

Foul Odours

The air is filled with foul odours
Which I try to ignore
I close my eyes
And form images and conceptions
I cherish
And let my mind wander
The man next to me
Seems utterly unaware of it though
I suddenly remember the fact that
'Women have a more acute sense of smell'
Odours go round and round in my head
I am determined not to give in though
But even my dreams seem
To have been impregnated with it.

Colour Of Compromise

Even white has become tarnished
On the canvas of the world
Don't you thing that
It's high time to add some colour to it
Basic colours are of no use of course
Complementary colours
Are what we need
To restore our health
And our salubrious past.

__Papa__

For the first time in your life
You did not put on your necktie this morning
How am I to going to console myself I know not
Your soul your eyes have turned snow white
O sycamore of venerable patriarchal look
You had reached spiritual perfection in the twilight home
Before you fell into your everlasting sleep
O time-honoured grandsire symbol of wisdom
You departed this life gliding
Without asking the support of anyone and
Causing wry faces around you
Now it's your festive occasion
Celebrated with loud hosannas

Patience

If you do not know how to be patient
Don't expect to partake of wisdom
Even though you enthrone in it
Don't expect to be conscious of it.

One

Harmony is within us
The voice is within
Even though we appear different
We are in line with each other
Look into you
There I am
Look into me
There you are.

Love

If you be a match stick
You are doomed to burn
Fall in with the eternal order and
Commit yourself to the flames of love

The cruellest of fascists and truculent leaders in power arise in a period when women and children are brushed off and this day and age progeny and future generations are crumbled under oppression.
~ Nuran Barengi

Last Act

I am a tree having its roots
Buried in the entrails of the earth
The more I penetrate into the innards
And reach the depths
With my branches turned inward
The more cerulean I become
I must feel in my bones the tree above
Reaching to the vault of the sky
In full consciousness of it
Blighted stems often canker
Life lasts
So long I breathe
The stage must go on, they say
Soon we must go
Till falls the curtain.

The Realm Of Love

While you were hunting for me among the planets
I had been searching you in every nook and cranny

While you drew your ships alongside the waterfront
Lading it with my poems
I calmly sipping my drink
Released my amniotic fluid to my heart,
To free my neck from the chord around my neck.

Under the planets equality has been denied to me
While the entire universe is at your disposal
I keep looking at my soul
In the hope of descrying your beacon
The universe has favoured me so
I came upon you in the end

I peeped through the crack of the door
Left ajar by those who had entered the path of love
And found in their virgin souls
Traces similar to mine

I know that my encounter with most of them
Instilled fear in me

I thought I went mad
In the seventh heaven that I was
I loved them all to distraction
Other times, other life styles, other loves
Yet same connotations and same significations
Annihilated in love
Our ashes merged into one
I blew a kiss
To the realm of the
Asexual love within me

Amour À La Mode

Panderers of moments
Who actually never experience them
If a poet keeps thundering
Without showering down rain
And composes verses
Chanting his love
Inscribing it on the walls
Without getting drenched to the skin
In the pouring rain
Its glamour is doomed to wane on the walls
Leaving behind but mournfulness and gloom.

Stain

Spattered with
Mock love stains
Like shallow pools of water
Striving to douse the sparkles of fire
Indelible grease stains are
Short- lived moments of love

Marriage Game

I play a game of hoops
With my love
At times I go a roundabout way
The hoop is the selfsame hoop
My love is my selfsame love
Yet it rarely reaches its intended end
I am synchronized with my love
My love becomes a stationary target
When the game ends
And I draw the curtains
Turning the day into the night
The hoop remains within my love

My Symphony

Good morning to the dawning day
In perfect peace
My head leaning on your chest
With steady heartbeats
Like a nursing babe
Notwithstanding
The din of jarring sounds

Ladybird

Teeming
Ladybird poems
We were not flowers
And they did not light upon us

Wine

A poem must not
Remain inert
It should like wine
Exhale the aroma
And the colour
Of the vineyard
That produced it
And when it matures
And the connoisseur
Takes a swig of it
It must bear witness to its time
Even though its taste
Acrid be.

My Stillborn Poems

Please don't worry
The scythe exercises its function
At every breath I take
I break one of the knees of my lines
And put off the coup de grace
Killing first their spirits and I ask them
"Your last will?"
"Can you recreate it in a fresh lyrical spirit?"
"No," I say by force of circumstances...
And then the decisive finishing blow comes
White blood gushes out
Spilling all over my invisible poems
Beaten
I return to the beginning

Confrontation At Mordoğan

Sound waves of Mordoğan
Stemmed
The tide within me
Effaced traffic line markings
Growing more and more distant
Unbeknown to anyone
Signs astray...
Waters that failed to keep company with you
Waters that were unable to keep company with you
Waters that were offended at you
Sources dried up
Balancing
Distorted lines
Monotonous
Daily dealings
Weltered in the sea
Striving for the shore
Lost is our former swimming style
Nevertheless
Splashing about in water
Make you feel all the same
Like a giant refreshed

The Narcissist

I have lost my gravitational force
My words, my dreams and my relations
Flutter about in the air
Like a cloud of dust
Who knows who will outlast
O you! O my poem!
O my love! O my narcissism!

Lesson

I browsed my way
Through faces lost in dreams
Cause of so many storms
Faces are the same faces
Black turned into white
In the window that altered
Wrath appeased
The game ended
All the money left to stake on one gamble
The white flag of surrender
Defeats
Are victories henceforth.

The Olive Tree
I

We are the branches of an olive tree
So long my sterility is transformed into voracious
branches
And I can reach for the sun
I don't care which season it is
Even though transformed
I find myself into a fruit
Let life prune me
As I please
Only an olive tree can pay
This blood money
I understand better now
So that our love
May henceforth
With a laurel wreath
Crowned be.

The Olive Tree
II

Half-brother branches
Of the olive tree
Grasped my arms
I hugged its trunk
In vernal equinox,
In autumnal equinox
Even though I've shut my face tightly
May life with olive bless me
Let us stand up to paucity of affection
And let my heart
With your love crowned be

Anxiety

Daily life
Marches on
Drilling holes
The stench of corruption
Sensitivity develops within me
In spite of appearances
When the curtain is opened part way
Sneaks in my life the systemized
What particularly concerns me is
That which is jammed
In a runaway system
Brake free vehicle
Tossing around
With destination unknown
Good things do happen though
The elation of one's child
Rushing to your arms
When back from office
Seduces me
While day
To evening.
Gives way

Istanbul, Don't Be Piqued At Me

Istanbul don't be piqued at me
It's true we've offended you
This is a fact
Lacklustre looks
In 'all' settled faces
On the outside of night
In particular
In a city where children's stony eyes
Scowl their disappointment at you
The recurrent dream of leaving it
For a vibrant
Scintillating city
Turn not your face away
When I charge at you
As I can't get rid of
The sense of being pressurized
I'll visit you again at my leisure time
Even though I am away
I shall miss you
In poets' poems.

Windowsill Flowers

I look at life
As though I were a windowsill flower
I don't know their names
If I have to be one of them
The name is not important anyway
It's the place it will occupy is important
I wish I were in a kindergarten
Bathed in sunlight
Even though I were a weed
I don't really care as long as
I feel above me their small feet
Trampling stamping crushing me

Submission

Of old

I tried to cling on to life
I was hurt
I was mortified
Unbearably lonely I felt
In the midst of the masses

Then suddenly you
Love like in fairy tales
Nay, even more so

Of old

I was a cactus
Trying to holding on life
In a sterile soil
Rarely blossoming

Then suddenly you
Out of the blue
Recalled to life I was
In your fertile soil

My roots clinging on to you
I clutched at you
And then at life

At times I may have clasped you
Too tightly perhaps
But, in the end, I
The cactus flower,
Yielded to you
With good grace

Projection

I wanted to write
My love to you
But I failed
Before me
Orhan Veli, the poet
Had already discovered
Just like Americus Vespucci
The inadequacy of words
To those who asked about you
I told them
You were the projection of God
The kindler of divine love.

Well formulated images are never obliterated and leave their imprints in works of perennial imagination.

~ Nuran Barengi

Nakedness

I no longer fear of
Being naked
Bulletproof and
Heavily armoured I am
With *Ruhver*
Against the world entire
In the past
In the unfathomed past
Like Don Quixote
Challenging the windmills
I was profoundly helpless
Although proud
The wretched loneliness
With revolver drawn
Came upon me
Although I took cover
Under the blanket
Too short to cover my feet
Stripped me stark naked

After You

When you were not there
There were insurgent
Mondays and Saturdays
And the 8th of Marches
After you
Every day has been
For me
The 8th of November and
The 22nd of September
When you were not there
I had my essays
And unyielding resistances
After you
My experiences
Have been transformed into
Poems
And attitudes
Tactfully tolerant.

One Heart

By thy side I was
At times monophonic
At times duophonic
At times cannon
But above all
One heart
POLY PHONIC

Farewell

I looked at your face
And saw farewell in it
I saw the grief
You experienced
Which you could not share
When I was not by your side
You wanted it to be kept
Like a photograph
Or a note
In a corner of a drawer
To be looked at now and then
Alas it's no more
I saw
In your face
The grief of loss
You experienced
I saw the farewell
Of a half-consumed love
Gasping for breath
Like a moribund

I saw the grief
You experienced
Which you could not share
When I was not by your side

Reproach

I am sorry
To have upset you
Thinking that I have upset you

Down with
The cause
And the effect
Of things I took for granted
And would have sacrificed my life
To justify their veracity

My senses
Have undergone mutation
Like the seagulls of Edirne

I reproach myself
At such moments
So much the worse
So much the better

I am confused
Full of regret
Yet, I am late again

And you haven't sensed it
I wrote to you
About everything:
Do forgive me
Will you?

Brush Strokes

Never experienced
I wish I had
I wish I were

Except those
Who caused me stray
From my path...

I thought it over
And gave it up

Had it not been for them...

Had I arrived
At the turning point of my life
At the other extremity

Before its time
Then, then
I would not be
Me

For the better
For the worse
Who can tell
The only thing I know is that
All the staging points I stopped at
Were the brushstrokes
That made me
What I happen to be now.

Anger

At times
When everything is OK
One feels offended for one reason or another
And flies into a fury
Like a storm suddenly unleashed
The dust swirls around
Like a misty cloud
An arrow is driven into one's breast
One's heart bleeds

Count in tens
If ever you can
Suppose you're in the right
Like all lunatics

All trouble comes from
Letting the cat out of the bag

Once you've careened down the hill
There's no coming back

Overwhelmingly defeated
One's heart contracts.

Cybernetics

I was but a kid
By some means or other
It must have lost its bearings
And fell into my lap

Stumped I was
I browsed and
Leafed through it
Perused it
I waded through it
I buried myself in it
And then
And then from beginning
I was lost in a daze

One thing I remember though
Only one single thing
Want to know it
Its caption
'Cybernetics'

It treated of cybernetics
An exact science most probably

I am not historically minded you know
So I forgot all about it
Except the caption
That fascinated me
Incomprehensibly

Mummy

It was the turning point
Of my life
The loss
Of my mother

I lost my bearings
In trying to understand
My life was spent
In mystification

Your absence has kneaded me
Shaped me
As your genes were within me
I owe my lingering beauty to them
Except that I have been a bit daredevil
You couldn't have anticipated could you
The fact that your absence moulded me

A poor little girl for ever orphaned
Had you been there by my side
I might not have been so offbeat

In your absence
I have never had the privilege
Of displaying my paucity
In your lifetime
We had never had the opportunity
To live exultantly
Many things have we shared
Yet I cannot recall any now
Your absence
Has rubbed me down
My leaven carried your genes
And I carried you within me.

Father

Old codger
The time has not come
Linger a little while longer
We'll go together
Sooner or later
Neither before
Nor after
O antediluvian patriarch
The alpha and omega
Don't try to outstrip the wind
Together we'll take the wing.

The Door

I shudder
When a door closes
Can it be because
I've never had a room of my own?
Can it be
Claustrophobia or
Some other phobia
Separation
Abandonment
Solitude
That's it!

Privation

A person feels bereft
When he's obliged to lead an ordinary life
Without being ordinary
A person feels penurious
When money is
Ever and anon
A person feels fleeced
When he feels the slap
Of bills on his face
A person feels
The persistent lack of money
At the end of the month only
A person feels bereft
When he must pull out
While he has things to do yet

Night

The day says adieu to the night
Silently, unwarranted
When dawn heralds it
Morning is ushered in
The day and the sun begin their rounds
Like it or not
The wandering soul
That lingered in the night
Descends upon the earth
At nights we used
To philosophize
Even on rug designs
At daytime
Depth was no more
So was philosophy

Black Market

Wherefore
This estrangement

Exchange of glances
Have become a rarity nowadays

Whence is this fear
Who knows
Why not acknowledge
My greeting
Its free

We were a warm-blooded nation weren't we?

Yet we find it
Frozen now
Cold is our entrails
Alas

God's salaam
Was freely displayed
In the days of yore
Now it has become almost

An object of derision
Rarely to be seen
In absolute necessity.

Kismet Selling Like Hot Cake

Painful expectations ad infinitum
A sad nothing
That often breaks the heart
Descry from afar as if out of reach
Yet so very near
Who knows
Maybe one day
It may smile at us too
Diminishing probabilities cry
For hopes forlorn
If only we had
At our disposal
The four-leaflets clover
Hidden in our pocket
The talisman for good fortune
The three apples that fell from the sky
Fell short of satisfying
The kismet
Selling like hot cakes.

Ankara- I

The first thing an Istanbulian sees
In Ankara is
The unseemly stone buildings
Deprived of sea sight
Bureaucracy galore
Ask me
What do I see in you

When I look at you I see
Warm friendship and
A house
Neat as a pin

A patriarchal attitude
Dignified
Yet
Modest and kind

Doors that can be knocked on
In the middle of the night

A dramatic irony
The unique city perhaps

Wherein money
Is not always
Value for money
The best part of it though
Is the presence of
Citizens alike in spirit
In rainbow colours
Warm as warm as can be

Ankara-II

In you
I lived the extremes
Soaring as in the fairy tales
And the platonic love
And the griefs that
Added depths to my life
The depths of the deep-sea divers
A single shot
Hitting the bull's eye

Ankara- III

You may become infatuated with
A city
Or even
Worship it
But in order to love it
You must have had a common experience
You have shared
With that city
Everybody
Bitter-sweet
Shares some experience
With a city
My beloved is you Ankara
And so is my experience

Istanbul

My buds have sprouted in you
Raconteurs have been in the right
You are one of those cities
That makes a man poet
Just like me

I'am No Poet

To those
Who hail me
Saying
What an idea
I am no poet
I've stolen the time
Of myself
And of those I loved
Poetry has been
Better than nothing

Acutely Sensitive Life Of A Poet

When a man pricks his ears to
The voice of one's senses
He is transformed into a creature
Totally different from what he actually was
And becomes a slave to his passions

He lives
As
A live bomb

Flooded
With tears
Yet I have never felt better
In my life

Why then
This
Dejection

When I hearken to my heart
I realize that
Unaware of the fact
That I have forgotten my inner voice

Now that I hear it
It explodes like a bomb
Scattering around pieces of torn flesh
And I am afraid of myself
Of my introspections
Life
Acutely sensitive of a poet
Marches on
Disturbing all one's balance
Without respite

Poetry After Forty

I am a verbose orator
It is my wont
But when I compose verses
I proceed with cautious steps
Like a perfume distiller

Converted are
Words
Into flowers
And
Poems
Into perfumes

But why after all these years
This sudden desire to compose
Poetry in which I never dabbled before

In order to write
One must replenished be
Replete with poetry to satiety
And go back to one's beginnings

Goddess Of Poetry

The poet
Experiences
Life
In its marrow
Why
I wonder
There are more male poets
Than female ones
While it's the female
That feels in her genes
Both happiness
And bliss
More than
The male
While
It's the female
Who
Draws water from the deepest wells
Whose experiences
Are the richest
And who procreates
Why does she not
Strike sail then

Responsibilities
That promise you days
Not to compose perhaps
But to be fully occupied
Prefer that you stay in the mainland.
The woman who prefers to remain in the mainland
May perhaps not compose verses
But can turn whatever she touches
Into poetry
Procreating
If she can
Engineer the process of birth
A solo experience
It's the woman who deserves
The attribute of
Goddess of Poetry

Faerie Poet

Lately I happened to write a couple of lines
And read a few
I have realized
That the poet of post eighties
Used a different language
Or rather he just scrawled
I feel like a soul
That after long years of sleep
In another world
Descended to the earth
Words are like
Concrete forms now
Which you can hang on the wall
And me with dilated eyes
Gaze at them aghast
And you
Elemental spirit
That have lingered
Until you've turned forty
You're all alone now
All other heavenly creatures
Having departed the earth.

Jerry -built House

To separate the day
From the night
These expressions
From a truck's licence plate
And have them
Perform dances
On different stages
Will be possible
Once the solar eclipse on my fingers
Comes to an end
The cause of my temporary darkness
O future poet
Is kept within me
"Design in poetry is a must"
Said the obligatory design expression
It's transformed in me
To a jerry-built house

Confrontation

I don't believe in coincidences
Hell and paradise I've seen both
I never regretted my past
I'm even reconciled with it
My pitiless myrmidons
Turning them into guardian angels
Who contributed to my verses

__Rain__

I feel oppressed
I feel distressed
Who may the culprit be
If not rain
Drizzling
Outside

Depression

When I compare today
To yesterday
The difference I see is
A darker or lighter
Shade in one
As compared to the other
And sometimes
Colourless altogether
What difference does it make anyway?

As time goes by
Free from tumult and disorder
Inanely quietly
Without producing anything
Relentlessly without respite
Recurring time endlessly
Passing away languidly

The clock
Please don't rush me anywhere
It marches on listlessly
No, I'm in no hurry.

Baby

Miraculous visitor
Descending upon the earth
From the lap of God

Believe me
This concentration
Can best be described
By tears trickling down within me
Kissable baby
That I dare not even touch

Nursing Mother

Suck baby suck my nipples
The pearl drops
The fruit of the union
Of the privileged miracle
With my soul
Let no one
No one
Interrupt this laudable process
Of which I am proud
And of which I am the designer
Pearl drops
That ooze for you
Smelling of paradise
In answer to my prayers

Lydia

If only you knew
What I'd been living through
These two years
When I had first thought of you
It was great joy
Hosannas and a couple of prayers from my memory
While within me chanted
Songs to joy
Symbols of my blissful day
As though I experienced it for the first time in my life
The highest prize one would be rewarded with

A Parent's Grief

I am in high spirits
How many mothers would fortune favour
I wonder
Enabling you to see
Your part and parcel
By the side of a mother

Maybe all of us
We are fruits of a deduction
But this is not so
Even though
To be able to see beyond
Is but a chimera

To find traces of his soul
We could hardly acknowledge his growing up
Let alone
Thinking him buried in the soul

An everlasting pain
Which has no beginning and no end
Change of the soil
Of a sprouting plant

Alas for the seed
Calcareous must have been the soil
A grief no one would like to partake of
If this is an exam
Flunk me Miss please!

Rehearsal

I cried so much today
As though I was rehearsing
A profound grief
I wept
Upset
And when I heard my sobs
Their wailing
Scared me
What if this were not a rehearsal I said to myself
The most primal fear
That of death

We miss so many things in life as we look in the rear view mirror.

~ Nuran Barengi

Orphan Kids Without Protection

Some of them are
Flowers in the garden
Some pussycats at home
Some attached to life
Like sprouting herbs
As though they themselves
Entered the path with no alternative
Like children without protection
Waiting for what only God knows
Can it be for visitors
To the vacant corners of their hearts

Adopted Orphans

When I think of them
My nipples ache
I cannot bear the sight
Of their plight
Some said that penury was
The culprit
Some said the environment was
The culprit
Some said the illiteracy was
The culprit
Some said fate was
The culprit
One said
Nonsense
The other said
You're talking through your head

I Want My Mummy

Why such passion to bear a child woman!
Why such insistence to have a child man!

The country's children are there
To wait on you and on me

There is an inflation of mothers there
Even though phony they be
Barely reminding of their originals

Hungry for exclusive loves
Where's mummy lulling me in her arms
The sleep of a mother
Hears even the flutter of butterflies

How sacred it must be
To nurse a child
Not the fruit of one's womb

Parenthesis

Woe to the parenthesis
Penitent parenthesis
Telltale parenthesis
Parentheses that
Guide one
At times
Egalitarian parenthesis
Parenthesis sometimes
An actor's action
On the stage
Parenthesis is history
Parenthesis
Mother of square brackets
Parenthesis
Dot dot dot
Parenthesis
Man of all seasons
Yet if it dies
No no one
Will know its absence

Growing Old

Solitude in old age
A quarter to the fatal end
The mere idea of it
Is a nightmare
Must one scratch one's back
By rubbing against the wall
Damn it! I'll hire a nurse
And it's the end of it
It's a lie
Money can help perhaps
Up to a certain extent
But what of the loneliness of heart
A permanent fact
Even though you start
Practicing your devotions
Can it help do you think
Loneliness is a scream
That pierces your deaf ears and
Sets your soul afire
You need the smiles and touches
Children's affection

Embracing your old withered body

To be loved must be
Nightmare for the lonely

Dream Line For A Poem

With mincing steps to old age
To the accompaniment of sparse sounds
Becoming once more a human being
With our boon companion thrombocytes
Now
The word raises its hand
For our lines that disturb our sleep
A charming faerie telling a tale
In which I have a fair share
Perches at night on my eyelids
But
But
I can't go to sleep
Just we said in our last line
Make way
For your REM sleep
And never give up following it.

Women Gliding from the Palm Of Life

The seagull that somehow manages to get along with
men
Along the shore line
Fly, o fly, as high as you can
Did you know that?
My intention was neither to touch the sky in which
you're soaring
Nor to hold you back
But just to empathize with your gliding in the heights
My feet hardly touching the ground
While I keep the butterflies in the pupils of my eyes
Lest my branches cover up their light
Anxious
Even though I am an illusion
In the lens of my umbilical chord
I hide myself
Scared that I am
Behind my eyeglasses
But
What's that smile on your face
I never saw before
Tell me Ingrid, do tell me

Rainwater

She washed her hair
In the rainwater
What about her entrails?
Grazed past the mould of humid fate
In her oubliette
If only she could get away
As half-baked single-winged liberty
Pervaded by the odour of childhood recollections
Transcending the woman she would be
For that future
For the sake of poems
She would kiss open her dreams
Even though fly we cannot
We can still swim in the rainwater she said.

A Father In Heart Of The Snow-white

A father in the heart of the snow-white
Carrying behind his back the entire sky
Where may he be going I wonder?
The eye cannot get accustomed to the white of the snow
Twinge of conscience
I peered and peered wondering the whole night
If one could put into a sack
The childish faces of Eskimos
Can there be such sacks such travels
Those who tortured the heavenly vault
What can I say
The avalanche fell
In the centre of the heart
A mother's curse
Dries up her milk
As they say
Heavens Muharrem
Once upon a time
And the date 6.02.2014
Diffidently I write
An avalanche fell
From the snowy long night

Absolution comes from the Creator
Of the intercessors
Interceding between
The child and the
Fair share

O Powers That Be

O powers that be
You've worn out my life
In this ephemeral world of ours
I go the way of all flesh
My sightless eyes
On my wings
Glued on you

Inspirational Message

Were I a tiny bubble of water
Clouds' ultimate essence
To fall upon the earth
Reaching the main
Having overcome all obstacles
Stretching out in all directions
Without let or hindrance
Being recast into billows
Embracing everything
Leaving out the nugatory
And proceeding on in my path
Deprived of any company
Counting out what I have experienced
Waking up to broad daylight
And realizing that
The sky is as blue as ever.

I Wish That Birds Flew Slower

As seasons and colours evolve and revolve
As cockroaches and glow worms increase and decrease
And everything in nature is formed and transformed
Change hands, hands ready to grip
Whatever I hand to them
Butterflies with transparent wings
Behind clothed walls
Our lost humanity
That litmus papers took the wraps off
In darkness and blindness
Are stored up our crudities
In momentariness of everyday life
You just can't say
Let's get down to our brass tags
As I am out of breath
I cannot find the emergency exits
Although all doors are unlocked in fact
Carved in our breast
Is our sluggish heart
Whose fetid breath
Is infected by untold utterances

Gasping hopelessly for liberty
Minority transformed into multiplicity
And sounds into screams
Go ahead bare us of our lives
Yet no tip shall be tendered to you
In settling of accounts
You shall wake up suddenly to see
That the past and the present are intertwined
Your pupils containing the resolutely insistent hope
Come on do give a name to this dawning day.

Relativism

Ô tessellated spirit of my country!
Uniformity strikes her with puerperal fever
Her travellers and innkeepers are never the same
Ô the butterfly paths that
Move in a series of leaps
My palm smells of onion
It takes more than a lifetime
To reverse the revolution
Of the simple present.

Red Necked Grebe

Amazon impregnated
Woman giving birth to
Cybele poems
How clever of you
To make one intuit
The path to common sense
That leads one to his soul
At every seasonal immigration
Your heart guides you to your dream world
Divesting you in the sky from your armour plate
And drifting you along to new poems
Carried by floods of springtime
Flourishing the refined hope
Infatuated with Turgut Uyar
And poetry's victim like Edip.

www.ingramcontent.com/pod-product-compliance
Lightning Source LLC
Chambersburg PA
CBHW071301040426
42444CB00009B/1816